#1 Best Selling Amazon Author

DAD's CHILD CUSTODY ACTION PLAN

INSIDER SECRETS TO FAMILY COURT SUCCESS

DAVID PISARRA, ESQ.

L

Legal Disclaimer

Hey Dad, this is a standard disclaimer blurb. I am just a lawyer. That's what we got to do. We (you and me) are not in an attorney client relationship. I am teaching you how to be your own lawyer, how to do strategy, how to do basics in the courtroom, how to introduce an exhibit, how to object to an exhibit, etc. This does not create an attorney client relationship. If you have a problem with that, go hire a lawyer.

Published by Libero Media, an imprint of
American Ghost Media

Ebook ISBN: 979-8-9924096-1-1
ISBN: 979-8-9924096-0-4

First Edition

DAD's CHILD CUSTODY ACTION PLAN

BONUS AUDIOBOOK!

Please enjoy listening to the entire text of **DAD'S CHILD CUSTODY ACTION PLAN** while you're headed to work, on the treadmill, walking the dog, doing yardwork or the dishes.

This audiobook contains the entire text of the Action Plan, the sample document Resources are available by download to your computer from your Library, once you log in to your account.

Just scan the below QR code, set up your **FREE** account, and download to your preferred listening device or computer.

Contents

DEDICATION

This book is dedicated to the fathers who are made to fight a battle they should never have had to fight. It's for the fathers who work two jobs, and then are told they don't do enough housework. It's for the dads who are denied parenting, while being told they only want more time to lower their child support. It's for the dads who go without so their kids can have more.

I see you. I respect you. I love you.

You're fuckin' awesome!

FOREWORD

What We Are Doing

Hey, Dad. For 25 years, I've been fighting for fathers in family court, and what I've noticed is this: men go into family court and say, "I'm a great dad!"—but then they have no idea what else to say.

This book is all about giving you the information you need so that you can turn to the judge and say, "Your Honor, I'm a great dad, and here's why." You'll learn to list off facts and information to support your argument, making it more likely that the judge will believe you when you say you're a great dad.

Unfortunately, Mom is likely to come into court and say that you are not a great dad. She may claim, "He's negligent! He doesn't know what he's doing and doesn't know the kids very well!"

What we're trying to do is give the judge two viewpoints. The first thing you need to understand about judges is this: they often think everyone is lying, and they probably are, to some degree. So the judge is trying to figure out, "Who do I believe? Do I believe Mom, who has all these facts, figures, and statements about what Dad is like, what the kids are like, and what they need? Or do I believe Dad, who only says, 'I'm a great dad'?"

If you were the judge, who would you want to believe? You might be inclined to trust Mom because she provides more information. This is one of the main focuses of this book: I'm giving you the tools to find and use the information you need to make a strong compelling argument to the judge and get what you want.

A father's strength isn't measured in muscles, but in the gentleness with which he holds his child's hand.

How To Talk To The Judge

One of the big questions people often have is, "How do I talk to the judge? Do I have to be super polite? Can I get angry with the judge? What should I do when speaking to the judge?" First off, remember this: the judge is there as a public servant. You must be respectful, but you can be assertive, and there's nothing wrong with being assertive. However, there is <u>a lot wrong</u> with being angry.

You do not want to tell the judge, "You are an idiot! You're not paying attention to me! You're not listening! This is wrong! She's lying!" That will make the judge immediately think you have an anger issue, which Mom will likely claim, and now you're proving her right.

The correct approach to being assertive is to say, "Your Honor, I respectfully disagree because I believe she is lying. Here's why I think she's lying, and here's my proof. You need to pay attention to this aspect, as it is important to the child and impacts the child's best interest in this way." That's the difference between being assertive and being angry. Anger will cause you to lose everything you want.

Witnesses

Next is how to deal with witnesses. Something that everyone wants, is to bring in as many character witnesses as possible. They want to prove their GOOD character, and usually to prove her BAD character. Often, dads may state desperately, "I have 43 people who will tell the judge I'm a great dad and how bad she is!"

See Sample Witness List in the Resource Section

Dad, you may only get one or two witnesses, and they need to be really relevant to the matters before the judge. More importantly, you must have them present in the courtroom. This is not one of those situations where you can simply call your mom and have her come down; that won't happen. If you have a witness, they need to be present that day.

You also need to exchange a witness list with the other side and ensure they are ready to testify. You should have your questions prepared. We will go into all of this in greater detail later in the book. But understand that you cannot bring in 43 people to tell the judge you are a great dad, 1) it's repetitive 2) because the judge does not have the time for all that. Remember this: the judge has 15, maybe 20 cases each day to deal with, and about two and a half hours to handle them all before lunch. Things move quickly in family court—except when they don't, as there are always continuances, but that's a different issue.

Exhibits & Evidence

A few words about exhibits versus evidence. This is a place where people often get really confused, and that leads to them being out of control. This is a very tricky area to explain, because there is the BIG PICTURE of EVIDENCE that iseverything that tends to prove or disprove a disputed fact, which includes testimony, reports, pictures, texts, emails, etc. When you are using one of those in a hearing or trial, the individual picture or text or email etc, are called "Exhibits". When in a hearing or trial Exhibits include everything you have: all of the text messages, emails, voice messages, school records, pictures, videos, etc. All of that is known as an Exhibit, and you can bring all of it to court to show the judge.

See Sample Exhibit List in the Resource Section

It helps to think of it like this, there's the big world of all caps EVIDENCE – that's everything you might use in your case; each part you want to use at a hearing or trial then becomes a capital E – Exhibits, like Exhibit A or Exhibit 23 etc. Once you've laid a foundation, and the Exhibit has been authenticated it becomes "Admitted Evidence" and now a court (the judge) can rely upon it when making a ruling.

Getting Exhibits authenticated is a process and to do that, you need to lay a foundation. Then, you must give the other side an opportunity to test that foundation, and finally, the judge must admit the exhibit into evidence. There is an entire chapter in this book that will cover all of this in greater detail.

But the short version is this: understand that there is a vast world of Exhibits the comprehensive collection of paperwork and then there is "Admitted Evidence", which consists of the few pieces of paper that you brought into court and that the judge admitted as evidence. The judge will rely on this Admitted Evidence to make a decision. If you do not present that evidence, the judge will likely rule against you. That is what happens in most cases: there is no evidence for the judge to rely on. You may have brought in a ton of exhibits, but if you didn't turn them into evidence, it won't matter. We will address this later in this book, and it's covered in the DADs Law School Evidence course.

See Evidence Script in the Resources Section

Cross Examination

You might want to cross-examine your ex, and you may feel tempted to be really aggressive in that cross-examination. However, I'm here to tell you that this is really the wrong approach. When you are cross-examining a witness, you are essentially telling your story through the questions you pose to the other side. We will cover this in greater detail later in this book.

But here's the short version: you tell your story in question format, such as, “Isn't it true that I have not missed any of my visits?” “Isn't it true that I'm always on time?” “Isn't it true that (fill in the blank)?”

They may respond with, “No, no, no!” but that doesn't matter. Do not get caught up in their answers, because their responses are not the real issue. The issue is: what story are you telling the judge? You are presenting the narrative that “I'm showing up on time, I haven't missed any visits, and they (mom) will deny it.” They will claim, “You are late all the time. You missed visits.” But if you have the proof—like the Dad's Daily Calendar I teach you to create, or receipts showing that you are actually doing your visitation—the judge can look at that and say, “Well, Dad has his calendar and receipts, while mom is saying, ‘No, he isn't.’ ”

This makes it easy for the judge to weigh hard evidence against a flimsy lie. This is how you prove that you are telling the truth, and the judge is likely to view mom's claims with a bit more skepticism because, while she says you aren't there, you have the proof that you were. That's why we use the Dad's Daily Calendar and bring in exhibits to turn them into Admitted Evidence.

Transcripts

Depending on where you live, there may or may not be an actual court reporter—that's the person sitting next to the judge with the stenography machine. They write down every word spoken by you, the judge, your ex, and any witnesses. You will want to order a copy of that transcript. Even if very little happened that day in court, you should still obtain a copy. The judge will frequently make their orders, and you want to ensure that the judge's orders are accurately reflected in the written records.

Order the transcript, which will cost you anywhere from $50 to $200, depending on how long your hearing lasted. This is crucial for you to have. Here's why: if mom said something that she's lying about, and you can prove it later, you want to be able to bring that transcript back into court. You can approach the judge and say, "Your Honor, last time we were here, she lied about this, and here's the proof." Of course, the judge will most likely NOT remember the exact orders, but if you have the transcript, you can submit it to the court and say, "Your Honor, last time we were here, on page 43 of the transcript, at line 12, she said this, but here's the proof that she's lying." Now you have something to use in court. That's why we order transcripts.

In the eyes of your child, you're not just a father – you're their first hero, teacher, and friend.

Kid Inventory / Proof of Relationship

One of the things you always need to prove to a judge is how good your relationship is with your child. The problem is that most dads go into court and say, "I'm a great dad," and you probably are, but that doesn't help the judge at all because every father who has ever walked into court has said the same thing. The judge has heard it from everyone, so it holds no meaning. You have to understand that it is what lawyers call "vague and ambiguous" – which means it has no clear meaning. In court the specific will always carry more weight than the general. You'll find that your opponent will often make very general or vague claims, and you can beat those the more specific you can be.

What helps is when you say, "I'm a great dad, and here's why. This is what we do, how we interact, how I discipline, and what I do when they have a meltdown." All of this information is part of Dad's Declaration and the Kid Inventory. These two documents are what we use to demonstrate to the judge the quality of your relationship with your child.

Your opponent is going to come in and say, "You do not know how to discipline. You do not know who their teachers are. You do not know who their doctors are. You do not know who their best friends are. You don't know how to do anything other than be a Disneyland dad." Great. Let her say all of that. What I want you to do is write your declaration using all the information from your Kid Inventory. You will use that to show the judge what you know about your child.

Your declaration will be your first impression with the judge; it is the first thing they will see about you. We often use this declaration and first impression to request more custodial time. One example might be, "I want more than just every other weekend and a Wednesday night pizza dinner. Here's why: I have this relationship with my child: we go to sports events, plays, museums, and we enjoy hot dogs and have fun together. We go to Chuck E. Cheese's and play video games or to John Potter's pizza place." Whatever it is, all of that information that demonstrates you are genuinely engaged with your child is vital. You will then tie that information with Dad's Diary, the calendar that contains receipts for all the activities you do together. This serves as proof to the judge that you are actively involved in your child's life and know them very well.

See Kid Inventory in the Resource Section

Another section in Dad's Declaration should include what you know about your child's school, their friends, their medical care, and how you discipline them. These are all ways we can show the judge a full picture of who you are as a parent. Because if a judge only hears, "I'm a great dad," you aren't saying much. When mom comes in and claims, "He doesn't know the kids very well," you can counter by saying, "I'm a great dad, and here's why." If you provide the judge with 10 pages detailing all the things you do with your kids, who do you think the judge will believe? We return to the credibility issue: what she says versus what you are proving. Proving is what matters. That's what allows a judge to say, "Okay, I see how this can work. I see that Dad is really engaged. He's willing to make sacrifices for his kids. He's willing to change his work hours and adapt his life. Let's talk about giving him more custody."

A father's love is the compass that guides his children through life's storms.

Ownership of Children Language

When you are talking to the judge, one of the most important things judges are trained to listen for is the language of ownership. Is it "my child"? "My son"? "My daughter"? Frequently, mothers use this language, and judges are very attuned to it because it indicates possession. It shows that they are claiming ownership of the child, and judges do not favor that language, as the reality is that children are the product of two people. What the judge wants to hear is a very subtle, almost subconscious indicator—they are trained to look for inclusive language. Are you referring to them as "our child," "our son," or "our daughter"? This language helps the judge recognize that you have a co-parenting mindset in place.

It is a crucial element because judges want to know that raising this child is still a team effort. Even if you and your ex are not living together, you still need to work together to raise the child. If you come in saying "our child," "our son," or "our daughter," while mom is saying "my kid, my kid, my kid," the judge is likely to think, "Who is more likely to help that relationship grow?" Will it be the possessive one or the inclusive one, the team player?

A father's love is shown in actions: in early mornings, late nights, and everything in between.

How To Lose In Family Court

Dad, you have to work through your emotions. Seriously. Get your anger out before you go to court. Custody battles are hell, and you will experience anger and rage like never before. Work through these emotions with a therapist, your best friend, or through writing. Consider going to a 12-step program. I don't care what you have to do. Whether you spend four hours a day in the gym or vent to whoever will listen at local bars, just do it.

You need to reach a point where you can walk into court and be assertive, but not aggressive. You don't want to go in and say, "She's lying, and I want my time." That will come across to the judge as anger, proving her point, and ultimately, you will lose your case. You need to be able to enter the courtroom calmly and succinctly express to the judge what you want and why. For example, say, "Your Honor, I think we should have 50/50 custody because…" and then start listing your reasons: "Here's how close we live, here's my work schedule, here's her work schedule, here's the child's schedule."

The goal is to have all of your emotional issues resolved before you go to court. If she triggers you during the hearing, you will flounder in anger, and you will lose. So please, do whatever you need to do to work through your emotions before you enter the courtroom.

Being a father means showing up every day, not just for the big moments.

Understanding State Law and Knowing The Family Code

In general, when it comes to family law, we are referring to state law. Unfortunately, federal law does not generally apply to cases in family court. The reason for this is that each state writes its own rules regarding marriage, child custody, domestic partnerships, and property division. So when you look at the law, you are really looking for your state's laws. You won't find the answers in the U.S. Constitution or federal regulations.

What you generally want to search for in Google is your state, followed by "family law" and then "child custody" or "child support." That's how you will find the information you need. Don't bother with the federal U.S. Constitution—such as "my pursuit of happiness"—as it won't provide what you're looking for. The federal courts do not care about these matters, because they are all state-level issues.

Dad, know your law. You really need to understand your legal rights. By that, I mean you should obtain the family code for your state and read it. You can find it online; just Google the actual code. The statutes are available for every state. The reason for this is that if you can quote the law to the judge regarding what you are asking for, you are more likely to capture their attention. Consequently, you are much more likely to get what you want.

For example, in California, if you have a restraining order against the other parent (the mother, in this case), you should reference Family Code Section 3044. This section states that the court presumes (meaning this is their starting point) that if there is a restraining order against the other parent, that parent should not have custody. It is not in the child's best interest for that parent to have custody unless they can demonstrate that they have been rehabilitated. The code also outlines what it takes for someone to rehabilitate themselves after a restraining order.

Every state has similar provisions. Each state has an entire section of codes, which is likely about two inches thick. This code contains the rules that will govern your case, and it won't take forever to read. Although it may appear daunting, it is actually more manageable than it seems. You can access it online for free—just Google your state and "Family Code," and you'll find all the relevant sections. When you know the code and can quote it to the judge, you will be surprised at how much more credible you will appear as a parent. This is also where you'll find the ELEMENTS that a judge must use when making a decision. For example, a judge may have to weigh the elements of the child's age, the parties distance from each other if one party relocated to a new state, and what's in the child's best interest; if you know the elements you can speak (write) to them and give the judge reasons why you should get what you want. But if you don't know what they're looking for, you can't give it to them.

When you go in calm, collected, and knowledgeable, you demonstrate that you know what you are talking about.

Through a father's eyes, every child is extraordinary.

Every Case Is Different

Imagine talking to your best friend Bobby, who also went through a custody battle. "I don't understand why I lost, Bobby! We both have kids. Neither of us is married to the mother. Why did I lose?" Well, most likely there's one fact—or maybe two—that are completely different between your situation and Bobby's. Essentially, you and your best friend could both have kids who are born on the same day. You have a boy, and he has a girl, but you have a substance abuse problem, while he does not. From a judge's perspective, this creates a completely different situation.

And that's the reality: one little fact can change everything.

Let's take another example: the same set of facts as above, but no substance abuse issues. You and Bobby are both good guys. You live 25 miles away from the mother of your child, while Bobby lives next door to his. Who's going to have more custodial time? Most likely, it's going to be Bobby. Why? He is closer to where the child lives than you are. That little fact, such as long distance, can impact things like pickup times and the duration that the child will spend in the car. Distance can influence a judge's perception of how difficult it will be for you to adjust your schedule to meet the child's needs. It's a small detail that can have a huge effect.

When it comes to family court, particularly in child custody cases, every case is different. I don't care if someone claims, "I have the exact same set of facts as someone else, but they got a different result!" Was it the same judge? Probably not. Judges have different perceptions and their own biases. You might have caught them on a good day or a bad day. The bottom line is this: you may have similar facts, and you may even have the same judge, but if one thing is different, you're likely to get a different result.

Understand that you are not necessarily guaranteed anything in family court, and one small detail can make a huge difference. This works the other way, too. One little fact can turn in your favor. For example, if your ex happens to have a substance abuse problem, you now have a much better shot at getting more time than Bobby. Mental health issues? You could secure more time if you can prove them and demonstrate that they impact the child—that's significant. Each case has its own facts, and you need to understand how those facts can influence the ultimate ruling of a judge. This understanding will affect what you should be asking for.

If you live an hour away from the mother, you probably shouldn't be asking for a 50/50, every-other-day exchange. No judge is going to want a child sitting in a car for two hours a day during exchanges; it doesn't make any sense. However, if you live next door or very close, you have a much better chance of getting what you're asking for. Again, you need to know how the facts of your case align with what you are requesting, and how likely it is that the judge will grant it.

Fatherhood requires patience, courage, and a willingness to learn something new every day.

Local Rules

When you are fighting for custody of your child in family court, one thing you need to be aware of, aside from the family code, is that there are often local rules. Each county or parish has its own set of rules. Wherever you live, that local division within your state will have specific rules regarding how to file a petition for paternity, how to file a response, how to request a hearing or orders, and the type of notice you are required to give to the other party, which means delivering the necessary papers. They will also have rules concerning how this process should be conducted, how many days before an event these actions should occur, and how long you have to respond once you receive those papers. These are the local rules.

To find them, all you need to do is visit your local superior court's website. Locate the court for your area—they will have their own site—and there should be a section labeled "local rules." This is a hyperlink you can click on, which will provide you with a printout of all the local rules. I highly recommend that you read them, as they can be very helpful when representing yourself.

Family Courts are open to the public, and you can sit in and watch. Occasionally the court may be cleared for a "confidential" case – usually that means a child is testifying so the judge clears the courtroom.

The next step is to enter the courtroom you will be assigned to and ask if the judge has any specific local rules, as each courtroom may have its own guidelines. They want things done in their own way, and we refer to these as the local-local rules, because they pertain to that specific judge. I also recommend sitting in and watching the judge for a day or two, before your hearing or trial so you get to know them, their demeanor. You'll likely hear arguments that are going to be similar to the issues in your case, and be better prepared to argue to the judge's bias.

For example, I had a case where the judge preferred everything in paper format. In Los Angeles County, most processes are going electronic, with everything displayed on giant screens and filed as PDFs. However, this judge is a bit old school and prefers to have actual paper to look at and make notes on. This method allows them to organize the documents more easily, with a pile for the petitioner and a pile for the respondent, helping them understand what is happening. While most judges today are not like this, each one has their own quirks and preferences, and you need to know what they are.

If you understand these preferences going in, you will be more likable to the judge, more likely to get what you want, and, more importantly, you will avoid making mistakes that could prevent your papers from being reviewed. You want to know these rules so the other side cannot use them against you. To recap, you have local rules at the county level and local-local rules at the courtroom level.

In the symphony of childhood, a father's presence is the steady bassline that holds everything together.

What to Look For In A Lawyer

Now that you've read why every case is different and how one small fact can have a huge impact on your situation, it's important to consider what you will ask the judge for. As a result, I want to encourage you to get a consultation with a lawyer in your district or county who truly knows what they are doing in family court.

Do not go to someone who lists 43 different areas of law on their website—everything from real estate and bankruptcy to personal injury and even "Albanian dog law." That is not the person you want for a consultation. Instead, look for someone with a minimum of 10 years of experience whose website focuses exclusively on family law. You need someone who fully understands the law in your state, how the local courts apply that law, and the likelihood that this judge will rule in your favor. You've surely heard the joke about the difference between a Good

Lawyer and a Great Lawyer – good lawyers know the law, great lawyers know the Judge!

A good lawyer can examine the facts of your case and provide you with a clear analysis: these are the strong facts, and these are the weak ones. They can help you identify what you need to argue against and how to prove that the negative facts are not as detrimental as they may seem. Guaranteed, those are the points that the mother will focus on. Every fact matters in a case, so getting a consultation with someone knowledgeable is crucial.

Pay attention to their insights and focus on the negative aspects of your case, so you can effectively neutralize them.

A father's wisdom grows not from books,
but from countless moments of choosing
love over convenience.

Do Your Homework

Here's a warning: if you're doing your Google research and your homework, as I've advised, and you're writing your declaration and your motions, please— and I mean please—do not rely on ChatGPT, Perplexity, or any other A.I. tools to write for you. You can use them for research and to help with organization and to spark ideas, but don't let them be the final draft your documents. Have AI create an outline, but then check all the references yourself. Make sure to humanize whatever is written, because a judge will easily recognize text generated by a computer. Trust me, we can spot that kind of stuff easily these days, and it's crucial that those references and case citations are legitimate.

A.I. has a tendency to fabricate information. There was a lawyer who, in a lapse of judgment, input something into ChatGPT, received a ruling, had an order drafted, and submitted it to the court with fake citations and fictitious cases. The other side discovered this, and now the lawyer is under scrutiny for submitting false information to a judge. They could even lose their license.

While you might not lose your license in a similar situation, you could very well lose your case. It's a bad idea to rely on A.I. for research in this context. Understand that you must double-check everything it provides by conducting your own research and confirming cases and rulings.

CASE NOTES: I had a client who was very involved in his defense against a Domestic Violence Restraining Order. He called me one night, super excited because he found a case with the SAME FACTS as ours, and the court ruled AGAINST the "victim". He sent the citation so I could use the case in our written arguments to the court.

If I didn't check the citation, I would have been using a made up case that ChatGPT had created. I could lose my license for that. You could lose your case, and your kids! Be very careful with the AI and research for legal documents.

Every bedtime story, every scraped knee,
every proud smile – these are the
building blocks of fatherhood.

The Kid Inventory

"Your Honor, I'm a great dad."

If you say that, and only that, in court, you are pretty much guaranteed to lose. What you have communicated to the judge is absolutely nothing. Claiming you're a great dad doesn't tell the judge how involved you are, how well you know your child, how you parent, or what type of parent you are. It's a very bland statement. You need to provide more detail.

I was at a Judges and Lawyers dinner, talking to a couple of judges, and I asked, "What's the one thing you want dads to tell you when they are in front of you?" Both judges said the same thing: dads need to provide more information. Dads need to show how they are engaged. Dads need to have reasonable expectations. Dads need to demonstrate what they are doing with their children. If they simply come in with a bold statement of "I'm a great dad," it is not enough.

The Kid Inventory, is a tool to help you show the judge that you are a great dad. Because I know you are—you just don't know how to prove that to the judge. You don't know how to collect and then organize what you need to prove that you are a great dad, that what the Kid Inventory is for.

Baby Proofing

We will start with the basics. Depending on the age of your child, is your apartment or house properly baby-proofed? It may seem silly to ask, "What parent isn't going to do that?" But if you can't provide proof to the judge—meaning you have receipts for the items you've purchased and photographs showing exactly what you've done to baby-proof—you're at a disadvantage. For example, those little plastic covers for the outlets need to be in place, and latches for the cabinets under the sink should also be installed. Take a picture of it and include it in your declaration. This will show the judge that you have properly baby-proofed your living space.

Why is this important? You might say, "I'm a great dad. Of course, I live in a safe environment." But the mother may counter, "I don't know what it looks like. I haven't been there. It's not properly baby-proofed. It's a danger to my child. I'm worried she's going to get hurt. I'm worried he's going to cut himself. I'm worried. I'm worried. I'm worried."

If you are the judge and you have a frantic mother expressing her concerns, while dad is over here saying, "Eh, it's going to be fine," the judge is going to have concerns. The judge is likely to ask, "Sir, what have you done to baby-proof your place? What have you done to show the mother that it's baby-proofed? What have you done to alleviate her fears?"

You might feel reluctant to address these questions, but you must do it to get past the judge. Baby-proof your home, take pictures, and send them to the mother so she can acknowledge, "I've seen them." Don't just send them casually; use email, preferably on Our Family Wizard or Talking Parents, so that there's proof that cannot be disputed.

If you must do it over the phone, that's fine, but make sure to get those pictures to the mother to demonstrate that you have baby-proofed your apartment or house. This way, she cannot say, "A, he never talks to me. B, I don't know what it looks like. C, it's not done."

Because if you can turn to the judge and say, "Your Honor, she's lying. Here's the email I sent her, here are the pictures I provided, and here's her response," what is the judge going to conclude? "A, Dad is doing what he's supposed to be doing. B, Mom is making things

TIP: Take a screenshot of the text to her with the pictures and submit it in your declaration to prove she's seen it!

up. C, Dad is arguing but not aggressively; he's being assertive and presenting his case, proving to me that he knows what he needs to do, he's done it, and he's ready to demonstrate that he's done it."

Car Seats

They are a big issue. When you have children who need to be in car seats, make sure you have your own. Don't rely on the mother to provide a car seat. Don't say, "This doesn't make any sense. Why do we have to have two car seats when we have one child?" Here's why: the mother will argue, "I shouldn't have to take the car seat out and put it in his car. He's going to take it, drop the child off, and I won't get the car seat back. Now I can't take the child to school because I don't have my own car seat. If he wants to be a parent, he should have his own car seat!"

Honestly, the mother has a point. Get your own car seat. What is it? $60? $70? $80? $120 for a really top-of-the-line one? Get your own car seat to eliminate this argument. It's a simple matter that can be easily handled. If you don't have the money for your own, check Goodwill; they probably have some. There are programs that can help you, like the Good Plus Foundation, which assists dads with necessities like car seats. Your local community likely has similar resources, and your friends may have extras. You probably know friends who have a car seat sitting unused in their garage because their kids have outgrown it.

Just get the car seat. Have your own. Don't tell the judge that it's stupid to have to get your own; just do it. It will make everything so much easier. If you have the proof, showing it to both the judge and the mother will help make those arguments disappear. That is the goal here: to eliminate the mother's arguments. The more we make them go away, the easier it will be for the judge to grant you what you want in terms of child custody.

Be a little creative in finding a solution to this problem so it cannot be used against you in family court.

Cribs & Separate Beds

Does your child have a crib or a separate bed at your apartment or house? If they do—and they should—you need to have pictures of that. You should be showing those pictures to the mother, and you need to present them to the judge as well as exhibits to your declaration.

Now, when the mother says, "I don't understand why you're sleeping in the same bed with him and that new girlfriend I can't stand. She's a tramp, she's a drug addict, she's horrible..." she is going to get completely off track, because she is upset and will try to use your new girlfriend against you.

But the reality is that it's all about the crib. If you have a crib and a separate bed, the mother cannot use those arguments against you. She may come up with other ones, but she won't be able to challenge this specific issue.

Your Own Diaper Bag & Supplies.

I know you don't want to buy your own diaper bag. Often, we think, "We have one child and one diaper bag. The diaper bag goes with the child. Why do I have to have my own?" But just like with everything else, it's best to have your own. It makes things so much easier so that she cannot argue against you. It's a simple matter, and honestly, it will probably be better for you because you'll know you have what you need.

Think about it: if you have to take the diaper bag from the mother and she decides to be difficult, you might only get one diaper. Now, what are you going to do? You'll have to take time out of your day to go to the store, buy new diapers, and restock the bag. Then the diaper bag goes back to her. Oh yes, those diapers are going back to her too, and she'll use them. Now you're paying for those diapers on top of the child support you're already providing. Get your own—it just makes everything easier.

The List of Emergency Numbers

This may seem silly, but honestly, it is vital. Do you have a list? A one-sheet document that includes emergency numbers for the closest emergency room and urgent care? What about the doctors for the child? Who is the pediatrician? Do they have a dentist? Are they old enough to have their own dental care? Do you have a psychologist listed? Is mental health included? Do you have poison control on there? Do you have the local fire department's non-emergency number? What about the local police department's non-emergency number?

Make sure you have a list of these emergency numbers and show it to the judge as an exhibit to your declaration. This demonstrates that you are prepared and have all the necessary contacts available. You may not be the one needing to use those numbers; perhaps it will be a babysitter or your mother trying to reach out to the grandmother or the mother of the child. They need to have access to this information.

All that contact information should be on one sheet. This sheet should be in the diaper bag, and it should be documented that you have shared it with the mother as well as with the judge. Again, this helps prove that you are prepared, on top of things, active, and engaged.

Parental Controls

The TVs, Xbox, PS5, your phone, iPads, tablets, computers, etc.—these are all items that need parental controls, depending on the age of the child. It's really simple to prove this to the judge. Set it up, snap a picture, print the picture, send it to the mother, and include it as an exhibit in your declaration submitted to the judge. It's an easy task that shows the judge, once again, that you are active, engaged, and proactive.

On top of everything else, this ensures that the child will not access channels on the TV that they shouldn't, and they won't get into inappropriate content on YouTube, and will not be able to visit adult websites. It's a good practice that helps counter the mother's arguments that you are not on top of things or that the child has too much access to media at your house.

Teaching Your Kids To Swim

So far we have covered preventive measures with your kids, but now let's work on the positive things you are doing with your child, like teaching them to swim. Have you taught your child to swim? Do you have pictures or videos of that? This is one of those activities that demonstrates you are active, engaged, and know how to interact with your child. It shows the day-to-day relationship growing and provides them with essential life skills.

Teaching them to swim, cook, play music, engage in art, practice carpentry, or learn metalwork—whatever is age-appropriate—are all valuable experiences. Make sure to back this up with pictures and videos. You are showing the judge how active and engaged you are, the bond between you and your child, and the importance of maintaining that bond. This helps demonstrate why you should have time with your child, and even more time together.

Disciplining

You want to show the judge why your relationship is important. You want to demonstrate that you are in love with your child, that your child is in love with you, and that you know how to raise and parent them, including how to discipline them appropriately. Part of this involves demonstrating to the court that you use suitable disciplinary actions when needed.

For example, if Bobby, who is six years old, has a meltdown in the grocery store, how are you going to handle it? Are you going to yell at him? No, that's not appropriate. Instead, pick Bobby up and take him outside. You do not shake him; you simply move him outside and separate him from the situation in a way that is least destructive to him and the surrounding environment.

Diary of Parenting

What are you doing each day with your kids? I suggest you get one of those big desk calendars that displays the entire month on one page. Each day that you have your child, mark it with a big note. I know this may seem silly or overkill, but literally write down what you did that day with your child. For example, "We made tacos yesterday, and then we went to the movie theater." The next week, you might write, "We went to a theme park and attended church on Sunday." The week after that, maybe you did something with Grandma and Grandpa. As you keep track of your activities with your child, make sure to keep your receipts.

The reason I recommend those big desk calendars is that when you have receipts, you can staple them to that month, making them easy to access when you need to go to court.

This is all important because it allows you to prove to the judge that you are using your allotted time to engage with your child. You are doing positive things with them, and you will have evidence to back it up.

Photo Book

Okay, Dad, a crucial piece of evidence proving your relationship with your child is putting together a photo book. This demonstrates to the judge everything you're doing with your child—the cooking, hair care, letting her paint your nails, games, building projects, whether it's models or Legos. All of that can be included in photos, and you can use the photo book to show the judge for two reasons: A) that you are actively involved, and B) who is in the child's life.

If you have pictures of the child at school, you can point out, "Oh, that's Mrs. O'Leary; she's Bobby's teacher. Oh, that's Mr. Johnson; he teaches Susie volleyball." This allows you to demonstrate to the judge, with verifiable evidence, that you know what you are doing and that you are engaged.

So when Mom says, "He never goes to school; he doesn't know who the teachers are. He doesn't know what's going on with the kid. He doesn't know what they like to eat," you can show pictures of yourself at school, pictures of the teachers, and pictures of you cooking. If you are cooking with the child, you probably know what they like to eat and what their food allergies are. Mom might say you don't know what those are, but here's your verifiable proof in the photo book.

The measure of a father isn't in his words, but in the character of the children he raises.

Step Up Parenting Plans

A step-up plan is just a way to introduce the child to a parent they don't have strong bonds or relationship with, so parenting time is increased to allow the child to adapt and adjust. (In my experience oftentimes this is not so much for the child as for the mother to adapt and adjust, particularly with first time moms who tend to be overly protective and controlling.) The purpose of a step-up plan is to address situations where you haven't had much parenting time with your child, and that's being used against you. You can address this specific concern in court by saying,

> **CASE NOTES: Here's the argument you are fighting:**
>
> **Dad asks,** "Can I get more time to parent the child?"
>
> **Mom says,** "No, you can't have more time, because you're a Bad Dad."
>
> **Dad asks,** "Why am I a Bad Dad?"
>
> **Mom says,** "No, because you don't spend any time with the child."

"Your Honor, I understand that I haven't been around much for whatever reason." (Whether it's been due to traveling, mom gatekeeping, or any other reason.) Acknowledge it, because the goal of a step-up plan is to help you get the experience of parenting.

Depending on the child's age, and how long it's been since you had regular parenting time a step-up plan can move quickly or very slowly. With a step-up plan, we will start with this month, or possibly the next two months.

Here's one example of creating a step-up plan: Initially, you will spend four hours with your child on Saturday. Then, the next month, or the third month from now, you will spend four hours on Saturday and four hours on Sunday. Two months later, that will increase that to eight hours each day. Finally, two months later, you will have your first overnight visit—Saturday morning at 9 a.m. to Sunday at 6 p.m.

The goal is to gradually increase your parenting time so that you can spend more time with the child. This is something that moms often dislike, and they may fight against it. However, the reality is that the judge is likely to agree to it because it is in the child's best interest to maintain a relationship with you.

So what if you haven't had much of a relationship? The way to address this is not to come in and say, "I want my 50% custody!" because judges will respond, "You haven't been around." Instead, you should come in and say, "I know I haven't been around. I want a step-up plan," signaling to the judge that you are aware there's an issue. This way, you are providing a solution and moving in the direction you want. That's why we use step-up plans. This is what it means when a judge or lawyer says, "We are going to offer you a step-up plan to help you get into the experience of parenting and build your relationship with your child over time."

The strength of fatherhood lies not in perfection, but in getting up each time you fall.

Building Your Credibility

We covered step-up plans and why they are important: because they help build credibility, with the judge, that's what we want to achieve. We want to build credibility at every opportunity. That's why I say the first impression you make with the judge is in your paperwork. The declaration, the response—whatever you file first with the judge—needs to look polished and thorough.

Building credibility is like constructing a wall. You lay down the first layer of foundation, then you build up a little more, and then a little more, and so on. All the while, you are demonstrating to the judge, "This is what I'm saying; here's my proof. This is what I'm saying; here's my proof." When a judge starts to see that pattern, they think, "Okay, I can trust what Dad is saying." Simultaneously, if we can point out areas where mom lacks credibility, we help to undermine her position and make the judge question, "Was what she said, really true?"

Remember, judges are observing mom on one side and you on the other, trying to determine, "Okay, who's telling the truth?" Both sides will slant the truth in their own ways, but the judge is looking for who is acting in the best interest of the child and who is more credible. This is where we need to step it up and really demonstrate to the judge. If mom says, "He doesn't know anything about the kids," you can respond, "Well, here is my ten-page declaration, Your Honor. It outlines what I know about the kids."

This is why we created the Kid's Inventory, and why we write in the way we do. All of this contributes to building credibility so that when you are in the courtroom in front of the judge and you say, "Your Honor, this is what I'm asking for, this is what I know about my child, and this is why I'm asking for it," they will look at you and think, "I got you, Sir!"

Through a father's dedication, ordinary days become extraordinary memories.

Co-Parenting Classes

One of the things I tell every father to do, whether you are ordered to or not, is to take a co-parenting class. You can do them online, and you can do them by yourself. They come in various lengths—six hours, 12 hours, 16 hours, 24 hours—whatever works for you. Just take one. It won't cost you a ton of money, and it won't take up too much of your time. You'll receive a certificate, which you can present in court and say, "Your Honor, here's my certificate. I've completed my co-parenting class."

Mom probably hasn't done this, or maybe she has. In a perfect world, you both would have better communication skills, as the goal of this is twofold. But in reality, she likely hasn't, and completing this class will help you build credibility with the judge. First, it shows the judge that you are proactive and taking initiative to become a better parent. Second, the certificate demonstrates that you are on top of things and doing what you're supposed to be doing, even if it's just a six-hour course.

This is likely more than what mom has done on her own. She may come into court and say, "I'm the mom, I've got the experience, I'm the better parent!" But she won't have anything to back it up. If you walk into court showing your co-parenting certificate, your first aid certificate, and any other relevant certifications—like in early childhood development—the judge will notice. They'll think, "This guy really knows his stuff. He's doing what he's supposed to be doing. He's credible because he's showing me these certificates."

I believe those programs are really helpful and the reality is that you're being proactive, showing the judge that you care about this situation. It's important enough for you to take action. So, I suggest you take a co-parenting class. It's online, it's easy to do, and remember to get that certificate to include in your declaration. When you do that, the judge will see you as more credible.

The greatest mark of a father is how he treats his children when no one is looking.

Parenting Classes

A co-parenting class focuses on your relationship with mom, while a parenting class is about you and your child. It teaches you how to parent in an age-appropriate manner. That's what a parenting course is for—it helps you manage challenges like your frustration during meltdowns in the store and how to discipline differently as your child grows. It's about maintaining your cool and developing your skills in relating to your children.

Co-parenting is about improving your relationship with the other parent. The purpose of a parenting course is to make you a better father. Let's face it: everyone can improve, and everyone can benefit from a parenting class. Taking one doesn't mean you're a bad dad; it shows you're an engaged dad who wants to enhance your parenting skills. You want to be a better father, and you're willing to take a parenting class—whether online or in person—to achieve that.

Most states offer online parenting classes that range from six to 24 hours. They are tailored to different age groups because what you deal with when parenting toddlers is certainly different from parenting pre-teens, and then there's the challenge of teenagers, which is a whole other topic. I believe in military boarding school for teenagers, but we'll tackle that in some other book.

The parenting class is for you, so you can walk into that courtroom and stand confidently in front of the judge to say, "Your Honor, I've completed my parenting class and my co-parenting class. I'm ready to be a more involved parent. This is why I'm asking for it, and this is what I want."

Every child needs a father who makes them feel like they can conquer the world.

First Aid Class and Certificate

You need to take a first aid class, and there's a good reason for it. When you're dealing with little children, they're going to get scrapes and hurt themselves. Having that certification is important because you include it in your declaration to show the judge. If you have teenage boys, you should update your first aid training, as teenage boys often engage in risky behavior. Keeping your certification current is crucial for credibility.

Showing the judge that you are proactive and take initiative demonstrates that you know what you need to do and that you are on top of it. Providing this information helps build your credibility and reminds the judge that you are a responsible person when you're asking for more time with your children. The judge is more likely to trust that you can handle emergencies.

So, go get that first aid class—plus you never know who you might meet!

A father's legacy lives on in the laughter, dreams, and courage of his children.

Support Network – Friends

Dad, you're probably feeling alone and isolated going through a breakup. One of the most important things you can do for yourself is to rebuild your support network. You likely lost a lot of friends when you broke up. My guess is that most of your friends were her friends, and they're probably not talking to you these days.

The old friends you had back in your bachelor days are likely wondering, "Dude, where have you been?" You might feel uncomfortable reaching out to them because you did what most guys do: you probably abandoned them for her. Now that she's out of the picture, you might think, "Hey, what are you doing?" and feel a bit awkward about it. That's okay—most men go through that.

However, it's important for you to rebuild that social network. You need a support system because what you're going through is really difficult. One of the best ways to navigate this is with friends.

The greatest chapters in a father's life are written in the smiles of his children.

Support Network – Family

When you're relying on your family, it can be tempting to vent about all the horrible things your ex did. You might think, "Did you know they did this? What about that? Don't you feel like I'm justified?" However, I really want to caution you against doing that. The other person will be in your life for a long time, and turning your family against them will only increase anger all around. It will also wear out your family if all you do is talk about the injustices, how bad it was, and how horrible the other person is. It gets old—quickly. So don't do that to your family, and don't do that to your friends. Instead, vent to a therapist.

You'll need therapy to have a safe place to express all that frustration. It's important to share, but be mindful of where you share. If you keep dumping everything on your family and friends, they will get burned out. You might start feeling awkward, and then you won't have the support network you need.

One area where it's important to grow your friendships again is through activities like gyms, work, sports clubs, bowling leagues, or baseball teams. These are all great ways to rebuild your support network. There's also another option you might not be considering: connecting with other dads, like those in the Boy Scouts or Girl Scouts, or whatever scouting organization your kids are involved in. There are other parents there, and you can reach out to them to build friendships.

Make it a space for genuine connection rather than just venting. Focus on rebuilding those social skills and having fun experiences for yourself, for them, and for the kids. This is all really important because what you're going through is one of the most devastating things a person can experience. You've lost your family, and you're not seeing your kids as much as you'd like. You're fighting for them, and it's costing you a lot of time and money. You're hurting, and people may be making assumptions about you based on what she's telling them.

You need to deal with all of that appropriately, which is why a good support network is essential. That's also why you need a therapist. I want you to get through this. I want you to heal and prepare for a great life with your kids. So go rebuild that social network, have fun with your friends, and get back to whatever you were doing before. You deserve a great life!

No New Girlfriend

Part of your support network may include a new girlfriend. However, I want to caution you against trauma-dumping about the old girlfriend to the new one, as this will only ruin that relationship. All you'll convey to the new girlfriend is that you're unstable, emotionally difficult, and a time sink.

Additionally, don't bring the new girlfriend around the kids too soon. By "too soon," I mean until you have permanent orders. Here's why: if you only have temporary orders, and you just broke up and have a new girlfriend, introducing her to the kids and wanting to do things together in an attempt to rebuild the family can backfire in a really bad way. The new girlfriend will likely upset the old girlfriend, and if this is happening in the middle of your custody battle, it will only raise tensions.

It can also be very traumatic for the children to integrate a new girlfriend (or boyfriend) into their world. Often they will feel that they are being treated poorly by you when they are in your custody, and take it out on the new partner. They really want to focus on you, and make sure that your relationship is solid since their world has probably been rocked pretty hard by the breakup of their parents, who they thought were going to be together forever.

Wait until you've gone through the process and have your permanent orders in place. Once you know what you're dealing with, then you can bring in the new girlfriend. Remember, introducing her too soon can lead to problems with the old girlfriend and potentially jeopardize the new relationship.

Fatherhood is a journey where the destination changes but the love remains constant.

Moving Party's Declaration

In a hearing or trial, there is always a statement by the party asking for the order. Sometimes it is called an Affidavit, or a Declaration, it should clearly state what is being asked for and why in language like this: "I am requesting full custody of our child because the child's dad lives very far away which makes commuting unbearable for our child" Why is that important? This is a statement that can be easily disproven if it false.

It may say, "the child's dad has an inflexible work schedule, working from 6 a.m. to 8 p.m. He can never drop off or pick up our child from school, nor can he help with homework."

Again, this is something you can contest, as you can provide evidence of your actual work schedule. Your testimony alone can inform the judge of your work hours. You could obtain a letter from your boss or a declaration detailing your work schedule. Additionally, you can show a map indicating the distances between your workplace, Mom's house, and the school, complete with mileage, to present to the judge. Your declaration can say, "She claims my schedule is inflexible, but my boss states I can choose my hours and I work from home, or I only work four miles away. This clearly shows that Mom is, at best, exaggerating, and at worst, misrepresenting the situation."

Mom's declaration may say, "the child's dad has no friends or family nearby to help." This can also be easily demonstrated. If you have rebuilt your social network and support system, you can bring in witnesses or obtain declarations from them to show that you have a backup plan. You can present support from your mother, father, best friend Joey, or anyone else who is part of your support network.

A father's love is the light that shows his children the way home, no matter how far they roam.

Responding Party's Declaration

The responding party's declaration will be titled something like "Declaration of Super Dad." At the top it should clearly state what you are asking for and why. Here your declaration can say you are asking for the opportunity to be as active and engaged a parent as possible, based on your current work schedule, the child's school schedule and their age. If you live only two miles apart it means commute time is minimal for the child. You can write, "the child can see her friends when she is with me because we all live within 2 miles of each other. My work is flexible, and I can pick her up after school, ensure homework gets done, or she can take the bus. My dad can also pick her up because he is retired and lives downstairs."

What we've done here is take all of the claims Mom has made and flipped them around, succinctly showing the judge why what Mom is saying is incorrect. As we dive deeper into our declaration, we will elaborate on these points to demonstrate to the judge that this is not just me saying it. For example you could say to the judge, "here's a declaration from my dad who lives downstairs, and here's a map showing that I only live five miles from the school and work four miles from there." These are all pieces of evidence we can present to the judge so that when they review both your declaration and Mom's, they will see that Mom made several allegations, and Dad addressed those allegations with solid Admissible Evidence. This will create a favorable impression, AND A LEGAL BASIS for the judge to know that you have everything under control, even if Mom claims he does not, and then rule in your favor.

The art of fatherhood is painted in moments of patience, presence, and unconditional love.

Get Clear Orders

One of the things you are asking judges to do is issue orders, and you want to be clear when making those requests. It is essential to present very specific requests to a judge, especially since you may be dealing with a mom who has borderline personality disorder. Your ex likely fits this description, which means you need to establish very tight boundaries. You have to be very specific: for example, "You will exchange the child at school on Monday at 8 a.m., and pick-up will be Tuesday at 3 p.m. at school."

When drafting these requests for the judge, you want to be as detailed as possible, particularly when dealing with individuals who have personality disorders like borderline personality disorder, as they will try to evade compliance in any way they can. The more specific you are, the easier it will be to return to court and say, "Your Honor, we have very clear orders. It states that I am supposed to pick up Bobby from school at 3 p.m. on Wednesday, and I was there. Mom had already picked up Bobby and wouldn't let me take him. That's a violation of an order, and I would like you to address it."

The judge may not take immediate action, but at least you will be able to demonstrate a pattern of behavior that shows the other party is not following the rules. This is why clear requests are important. If you simply state, "You are supposed to pick up the child on Wednesday," that leaves too many questions: Where was the child supposed to be? At home, at her house, at school, or after soccer practice?

You want to ensure everything is very specific because this will make your life easier in the long run. While it may take more effort to think things through at the beginning, you will be grateful on the back end for having a clear order and a well-defined request made to the judge.

Being a father means having your heart walk around outside your body.

Your Papers Are Your First Impresssion

Your declaration creates your first impression. The other documents you will have at your hearing or trial—whether they are exhibits, videos, or examples of text messages you've printed out—need to be properly organized. This way, you can easily access them when you need to use them, especially since you must show them to the other side. Before the hearing, the court will ask if you have shown your exhibits to the other party to avoid any surprises.

You want to have everything organized so that when you ask the judge to admit them into evidence, you can quickly retrieve them, use them with a witness, establish a foundation, and have them admitted into evidence. This ensures the judge can rely on them when making decisions. This topic is covered in detail in the Evidence course, which you have access to when you become DADs Law School VIP member.

The greatest gift a father can give his children is believing in them before they believe in themselves.

Dress For Success

We know that the first impression we make with the judge is through our written papers. The second impression comes when you actually walk into the courtroom, and this is where dressing for success matters. Do you have to show up in a tuxedo and top hat? No. Do you need to wear a suit and tie? No. You do need to arrive clean and properly dressed, perhaps in a collared shirt and clean pants, to demonstrate that you respect the court. Yes, that's what it means to dress for success. You simply need to show up and convey to the judge that you are ready for business by being properly dressed for who you are as a man.

That doesn't necessarily mean a suit and tie; if you're the kind of person who wears a collared shirt, then wear a clean collared shirt and perhaps have your pants pressed. The important thing is to arrive prepared and present yourself as properly. This is crucial, as it forms the second impression you will make on the judge.

I've seen people show up to court in flip-flops, gym shorts, and tank tops. It did not go well; the judge is unlikely to respect someone who dresses like that as much as they would respect someone who arrives in a polo shirt, clean jeans, and decent shoes. The message sent is different. It communicates, "I am respectful of the judge, I recognize your authority, and I value these proceedings. This is important to me." All you need to convey is that "Your Honor, I'm taking this seriously, and I'm showing you that by the way I'm dressed."

The best inheritance a father can leave his children is the example of a life well lived.

Public Speaking

When speaking to the judge, many people feel scared; it's a very intimidating situation. The future relationship with your children is at stake, and you have only a limited amount of time. You're probably not a professional speaker and likely don't frequently appear in front of judges. One way to enhance your presentation is to have a script. Prepare a case statement—a short introduction that says, "Your Honor, this is who our family is. I'm sure you have read our papers. Here's what I'm asking for, just to reiterate, and here's why."

Having something prepared makes it easier to communicate with the judge. Once you get into the flow, I guarantee you'll be okay, but you need to overcome that initial hurdle of, "Oh my God, I have to talk to the judge." If you have a short paragraph written out beforehand, it will help you find your rhythm, gain some momentum, and feel more comfortable during your conversation with the judge.

See Evidence Script in Resource Section.

Additionally, you have our evidence scripts. An evidence script will assist you in getting a piece of evidence admitted to court. You'll take an exhibit, have it marked and identified, and offer it to the other side. You will need to lay a foundation for the exhibit by having a witness testify to its accuracy and authenticity. They answer the questions of What, Where, When, Why, and How etc. Once a foundation has been laid for the exhibit you will then say, "Your honor I'd like to offer this exhibit into Evidence." The judge will then ask if there are any objections. They will say yes or no. If there are no objections then the judge will admit it into evidence, and now you have Admitted Evidence.

If you are familiar with those scripts for text messages, pictures, videos, and emails, it will make your life much easier in court. You'll know the answer when you want to use these text messages where she called you a jerk and are asking, "How do I get those into evidence?" With a script, you can do just that. Once it's admitted, the judge can rely on it to see, "Oh, Mom's being abusive to Dad, and here's the proof." This approach can lead to a different outcome in family court, as it shows the other side lacks credibility or is abusive. That's how you win: by getting evidence in, that illustrates these points.

When you speak, nerves can take over; you might find yourself talking quickly and forgetting to breathe because you feel you need to share everything at once. It's crucial to remember that you will have the time to speak to the judge. Breathing allows the other party to think and process what you just said. Your pauses give them a chance to understand your message.

It's vital for both of you. You need to slow down for several reasons—one being that there's likely a court reporter taking everything down and they have a limit on what they can record. They're fast, but you can still speak too quickly for them. Also if you speak too quickly, the judge may not grasp all the information. They can only process your words if you take a moment to breathe.

Remember, when you speak in front of a judge, your adrenaline will be high. You might experience a dry mouth and a racing heart. It's okay to pause and breathe. When adrenaline kicks in, it will compress your perception of time. If you take a three-second breath, it may feel too long to you, but it gives the other side a chance to consider what you just said. It allows you to gather your thoughts, take in some oxygen, and calm down. Do it now, just breathe and count, One Mississippi, Two Mississippi, Three Mississippi. It's not that long in reality is it?

Breathing is crucial in public speaking; it benefits both the speaker and the listener. Don't be afraid to pause; it's perfectly fine. One aspect to be mindful of is filler words, such as "um," "uh," and "you know." Being aware of these can improve your delivery. If you practice your speech and reduce those filler words, you'll come across as more credible and less nervous, which will likely lead to a better outcome in front of the judge. Don't worry about getting rid of all of them. Even the best public speakers have them at times. The point is just to bring focus to what you are saying so that you express yourself to the judge.

A father's arms might be tired, but his heart never grows weary of loving his children.

Exhibits Vs Evidence

One of the most important things you need to understand is the difference between exhibits and evidence. It can be a bit confusing because there's a broad category called EVIDENCE. When you see it in all capitals like that what I mean is everything that could possibly be used in a trial, think of it like a giant umbrella that is everything— witnesses' testimony, text messages, voicemails, emails, school records, doctor's notes, calendars, receipts, and more. All of that can be classified as EVIDENCE. Each individual piece, such as a single text message or email, is considered an Exhibit. An exhibit is just one piece of information that you will use to either prove or disprove an element of your case—essentially, to show the judge whether the other side is correct in claiming that you did or didn't do something.

Remember that each piece in the big pile of EVIDENCE becomes an Exhibit through the testimony of witnesses or experts. For example, you may have an email from school about your child being late too many times and you want to use to prove to the judge that Mom's always late to school but you're not. You would Mark and Identify it, then lay a foundation for it by having Mom testify that she got a copy of it and yes her email address is in the "To:" section and this is an accurate copy of the email.

If someone left you a voicemail, that can also serve as an exhibit. Usually you will need to have a transcription to make it easier for the judge to understand what is being said, and you'll play it in court. You'll testify that this message was left on your phone, and that voice is the Mom and you recognize it, plus what she says identifies her as the Mom.

You may also want to use photographs of you and your child, or simulations such as a map showing where you live, where Mom lives, where the child goes to school, and where you both work, can all be valuable. This creates a visual representation of the logistics of your case.

Then there are depositions. If you have deposed the other side, that's where a person makes a statement under penalty of perjury, it can be used at trial if they contradict what they said in the deposition. Sometimes, you may conduct reconstructions, especially if there are allegations of domestic violence, to explain to the judge what really happened. Similarly, you can use models.

Exhibits start the process to become evidence once they are marked and identified. Here's how it works: you take an exhibit, like an email, and say, "Your Honor, I'd like to mark and identify Respondent's Exhibit Number One, which is an email from Mom to Dad, dated June 2, 2023." At this point, it is officially marked as Respondent's Exhibit One. You can either place a sticker on it indicating "Exhibit One" or mark the back of it. This helps the clerk keep track of which exhibit markers have been used, allowing the judge to decide which exhibits to rely on when making a ruling. These should match the exhibit markers you used when you submitted your Exhibit List in the pre-trial preparation.

> **PRACTICE POINTER:**
>
> **Often lawyers prior to a hearing or trial, will agree that all identified exhibits will be admitted. This is done to save time and avoid having witnesses lay foundations for basic documents like emails and texts that everyone has.**

When an exhibit is used into evidence, it means it was marked and identified as for example, Respondent's Exhibit One. Next you would lay a foundation for the Exhibit and offer it into evidence by stating, "Your Honor, I'd like to offer Respondent's Exhibit One into evidence." The judge then asks the other side if they have any objections, and if they say "no objection," the judge will "move it into evidence" and now they can rely upon it.

For example, if you want to admit an exhibit as Respondent's Exhibit One, after you have Marked and Identified, and a foundation has been laid for it, you say, "I'd like to offer Respondent's One into evidence," the judge will turn to the other side and ask if there are any objections. If they say, "Yes, we object. Lack of foundation," that means there has not been enough testimony verifying whether this email is accurate or a true copy, and how we know it is authenticated.

PRACTICE POINTER: IMPEACHMENT EVIDENCE.

Impeachment evidence is not shared with the other side in either your Exhibit List or in the Exchange of Exhibits that some judges want you to do prior to trial/hearing. This is how you catch the other side in a lie and get them thrown off their game. You set them up to answer a question that you know they will lie about, and then you introduce the Impeachment Exhibit that proves they are lying.

To establish this foundation, you would have Mom on the witness stand and ask, "Do you recognize Exhibit One?" Mom would respond, "Yes." Your follow up question is, " Is this an email from you to David?" Then, she would say, "Yes,." Your next statement is "Your Honor, I'd like to offer this into evidence." Once Mom recognizes and agrees it is what you say it is, you have laid the foundation, and the judge would then admit it into evidence now that you have established its authenticity.

The heart of a father is where his children find their beginning and their endless possibilities.

Witnesses

You will likely have a number of witnesses you want to bring in, ranging from your child's kindergarten teacher to their senior prom tuxedo rental shop owner. However, that's not realistic; you will probably have two, three, or maybe four witnesses at most for most cases.

To handle witnesses properly, you need to create a witness list. This list shows the other side who your witnesses will be and informs the court as well. We've provided you with a sample witness list, which is a basic document consisting of four columns: the witness's name, a brief explanation of what you expect them to testify about, an estimate of how long you think they will be on the witness stand, and a short description of why they are relevant to your case.

For example, you might have Grandma come in to testify about how often she sees the child, what kind of daycare she provides, her home environment, and her availability. You would estimate how long Grandma will be testifying and prepare your questions accordingly.

You may also want to bring in your boss to testify about your work availability. Is your work schedule flexible? Do you work from home? How accommodating is your company when it comes to taking time off if your child is sick? These points are important, especially if Mom has claimed that you are a terrible parent who cannot have custody due to an inflexible work schedule. Your boss can confirm that it is, in fact, quite flexible and that your company is family-friendly.

If Mom says you are not available to assist with school activities, you can bring in the child's teacher to demonstrate that you have a good relationship with them. You might mention that you have participated in classroom activities, such as "Daddy Day," or that you have chaperoned field trips.

See Sample Witness List in the Resource Section.

Additionally, you could bring in the child's grandparent and perhaps one of your fellow Scout leaders to counter Mom's claims. These witnesses will help show that Mom was either lying or at least exaggerating about your involvement and capabilities as a parent.

Fatherhood is about the moments that seem small but build foundations that last forever.

Direct & Cross Examination

When you have your witness on the stand and you are asking them questions, this process is called direct examination. Direct examination involves asking questions like, "Can you explain what's going on here?" or "Can you tell me why something happened?" For example, if you are examining your boss, you might ask, "Mr. Boss, how flexible is the company regarding working from home?" Mr. Boss would then respond, "We are an extremely flexible company. Half of our employees work from home on an alternate schedule."

The purpose of direct examination is to tell the story of what you want the judge to know. You ask open-ended questions that allow the witness to provide detailed answers. You want them to tell the judge your story through their voice and observations, such as grandparents discussing their availability, employers describing the company's family-friendly policies, or teachers noting your involvement at school.

When Mom brings in her witnesses, she may call friends, neighbors, or her boss. The approach to dealing with Mom's witnesses is different because this process is called cross-examination. During cross-examination, you aim to tell your story through the way you ask questions. You want your questions to elicit yes or no answers, avoiding long, extensive responses.

For example, you might ask, "Isn't it true that you, Mom's friend, were with her when she received her DUI on June 5, 1993?" or "So, you are an alcoholic also, aren't you?" You could also ask, "You're the one who caused her to have that car accident when you grabbed the wheel, right?" This line of questioning allows you to convey your narrative about Mom and her friends while challenging their credibility.

For instance, you might ask Mom's neighbor, "Isn't it true that you are hard of hearing?" This question succinctly makes your point. The way you frame your questions is crucial during cross-examination because it helps you communicate your story to the judge through those questions.

A father's footsteps leave a path for his children to follow, even when he's no longer walking beside them.

Order A Transcript

At the end of a hearing, I highly recommend that you obtain a copy of the transcript if a court reporter was present. The court reporter has been there to record every word spoken, hopefully. The reason we want to have a transcript is twofold: first, to ensure that what the judge ruled is accurately reflected in the order; and second, if Mom said something that we plan to use against her in a later hearing, we want to have that transcript. If she lied during this hearing and then contradicts herself later, we want to be able to show the judge that she is lying in one instance or the other, or possibly both.

To order a transcript all you have to do is at the end of day of the trial or hearing, just approach the stenographer / court reporter and tell them you want a copy of the transcript. They'll ask you for contact information so they can be paid. Usually it's about a $1.50 a page in Los Angeles right now. They will let you know how long it will be before they are done with the transcript.

Fatherhood is the greatest growth opportunity a man will ever have. It's the most meaningful relationship in his life, which creates his true legacy.

CONCLUSION

Next Steps and Final Thoughts

All right, that wraps up the Child Custody Action Plan. You now have some great tools to go and fight for your child and your parenting time. You know your kid, you know what you mean to them, and how important it is for you to show up, and now you know how to prove that to the judge so you can get the parenting time you want and they deserve.

Your next steps are to

1. Prepare your case statement, (sometimes called a Trial Brief)
2. Compile your Kid Inventory,
3. Create your Witness List,
4. Create your Exhibit List and
5. Prepare your Exhibit Books (you'll need 4 of them, one for you, one for the judge, one for the witness and one for the other side)

6. Determine your requests and the reasons why it is in your child's best interest.

I suggest you consult with a local attorney for local law and information on your judge. Knowing how they generally rule can help you give them what they need to find in your favor.

If you want help, at DADs Law School our VIP Members have access to our online video courses for all of this, plus our twice a month Meetups to go over your questions and concerns. You can learn more about it here: www.DadsLawSchool.com.

There's a lot at stake here, and I know you probably have a lot of anxiety, that's why I wrote this book, do my videos, created DadsLawSchool, host DADs Badass Bootcamps, and lead the meetups. Helping Dads navigate these rough seas is important to me. I'd love to have you come join us and get the support you want and need.

It's a difficult process that you are facing. It's emotionally draining. It's physically exhausting. If you have lawyers involved, it's financially a nightmare. But you're not alone. Each year about a million men become dads and enter the court system through either the Child Support Collection Agencies, or the Family Courts as they fight to have time with their kids. It's a sad statement on our society that Dads are made to fight for time with their kids, but child support is so easily granted to moms.

I know you want to be a big part of your kids life. You wouldn't be reading this if you didn't. The fact that you are seeing this tells me a huge amount about who you are as a father, as a man, and as a warrior. I want to let you know that you are

- Seen
- Respected
- And you are loved.
- I see you.
- I respect you.
- Your kids love you.

Lastly I love you. I love you for all of the reasons above plus, you are standing up in a system that is hard to navigate and defaults to easy answers, simple decisions and ignores lies.

Best wishes and remember that I think You're Freaking Awesome!

David

RESOURCES

Each of the following documents are available to you when you become a VIP member of DADs Law School, along with the video courses that accompany them. To become a member go to www.DadsLawSchool.com or scan this QR code:

- Super Dad Declaration
- Exhibit List
- Witness List
- Exhibit Cheat Sheet
- Kid Inventory

Dedicated Dad
1 Engaged Father Way
Parenthood, Mars

In Pro Per / Pro Se

COUNTY OF DEVOTION
STATE OF HARD WORK

IN RE	)	
	)	FILE NO:
DEDICATED DAD	)	
PETITIONER	)	DECLARATION OF
	)	DEDICATED DAD
v.	)	
CLAIR DE LUNE	)	
RESPONDENT	)	
	)	
	)	
	)	

I.

1. I, DEDICATED DAD HEREBY DECLARE I am over the age of 18 and submit the following as an offer of proof as to what I would and could testify to:

II.
REQUESTED ORDERS:

2. THIS IS WHAT I'M ASKING FOR AND WHY:
    a. THE OPPORTUNITY to be as active and engaged as a parent as possible based on my work schedule, the child's school schedule and age.
    b. We live only XX miles apart – which means commute time is minimal for the child
    c. The child can see her friends when with me, because we all live close enough.

d. My work is flexible and I can pick up after school and make sure homework gets done. OR they take the bus, or my Dad can pick them up because he's retired and lives downstairs….
e. I can drop off at school because it's on my way to work. OR my mom can drop the child off at school, or there's a bus that picks them up…
f. I want every 1st, 3rd and 5th weekend because that will allow me time to bond and do weekend activities with our child. If we split the weekends, we each get time with our child and time alone.
g. I want us each to have a 2 week summer break to travel because those experiences enhance the bonding between child and parent.

III.
HERE'S WHY I'M A GOOD PARENT:

a. THE BASICS – I HAVE ALL THAT I NEED TO TAKE CARE OF MY CHILD IMMEDIATELY
    i. HOUSE/APARTMENT IS BABY PROOFED
    ii. CAR SEATS BASED ON AGE/WEIGHT
    iii. CRIBS
    iv. HIGH CHAIRS
    v. DIAPER BAG AND SUPPLIES (YES GET YOUR OWN!)
    vi. BED AND BEDDING
    vii. HAVE ALL EMERGENCY NUMBERS ON THE FRIDGE – POISON CONTROL, PEDIATRICIAN, I KNOW THE LOCAL EMERGENCY ROOM AND WHERE IT'S AT
    viii. PARENTAL CONTROLS ON TV/ COMPUTERS /
    ix. TAUGHT KID HOW TO SWIM (IF THERE IS A POOL NEARBY)
b. CALENDAR OF CUSTODY / DIARY OF PARENTING
c. PHOTO BOOK
    i. SCHOOL STUFF

    ii. ACTIVITIES WITH THE KIDS
    iii. YOUR HOUSING - **ESPECIALLY THE SLEEPING ARRANGEMENTS**

  d. RECEIPTS
  e. STEP UP BEFORE YOU TRY TO STEP IN - PROVE YOU'RE ENGAGED BY **YOU** REACHING OUT TO THE SCHOOL, DRs, ETC. KEEP THE PROOF, DATES, MESSAGES LEFT, EMAILS SENT.

(NOT MOM'S JOB TO KEEP YOU UP TO DATE – BE PROACTIVE!)

1. **CLASSES I'VE TAKEN TO BE A BETTER PARENT AND CO-PARENT**
    a. **CO-PARENTING CLASS** – You can take a class WITHOUT your ex, you can take one with her, you can take them separately. This is about your communication skills with her. (Exhibit 1 – Completion certificate)
    b. **PARENTING CLASS** - This is about your relationship with your children – developmental ages, behavior modification etc(Exhibit 2 – Completion certificate)
    c. **1ST AID** – basics of dealing with bleeding boys primarily. (Exhibit 3 – Completion certificate)
2. **THE SUPPORT NETWORK I HAVE TO HELP ME.**
    a. **FAMILY** – who is there to help you with daycare, instill values and back you up on your custodial days
    b. **FRIENDS** – who is there to help you, but also to demonstrate to your kids that you have a social life and friends, so you can model appropriate behaviors
    c. **NEW GIRLFRIEND** – danger Will Robinson DANGER!!! Odds are this will spike her anger and she'll demand that you never allow your child to be around that skeezy slut you're dating…
    d. **SCOUTS/CHURCH** - what are the social groups you're a part of?
    e. **THERAPY** – yep, you should at least get into a few sessions to see why it didn't work out with the ex. You

can call me, but seriously at $695/hour do you really want to go over your relationship choice issues with me?

3. **THE LOGISTICS OF HOW I THINK IT CAN WORK AND WHY.**

a. PROXIMITY

b. MAP IT OUT

    i. CREATE A GRAPHIC SCHEDULE FOR THE JUDGE

4. **THIS IS WHAT I'M ASKING FOR AND WHY:**

    a. THE OPPORTUNITY to be as active and engaged as a parent as possible based on my work schedule, the child's school schedule and age.
    b. We live only XX miles apart – which means commute time is minimal for the child
    c. The child can see her friends when with me, because we all live close enough.
    d. My work is flexible and I can pick up after school and make sure homework gets done. OR they take the bus, or my Dad can pick them up because he's retired and lives downstairs....
    e. I can drop off at school because it's on my way to work. OR my mom can drop the child off at school, or there's a bus that picks them up...
    f. I want every 1st, 3rd and 5th weekend because that will allow me time to bond and do weekend activities with our child. If we split the weekends, we each get time with child and time alone.
    g. I want us each to have a 2 week summer break to travel because those experiences enhance the bonding between child and parent.
    h. MAKE IT EASY FOR THE JUDGE TO GIVE YOU WHAT YOU WANT

I declare the foregoing to be a true and correct statement under penalty of perjury, according to the state of HARD WORK.

DATED:

____
SUPER DAD

DAFFY DUCK
In Pro Per
213 Main Street
Neverland, OZ, 420365

SUPERIOR COURT OF OZ
COUNTY OF ABSURDITY

DAFFY DUCK *Petitioner*	} **Case NO: 19VEPT2016**
VS.	} **PETITIONER'S EXHIBIT LIST and EXHIBIT LINK**
DAISY DUCK *Respondent*	}

I.
PETITIONER'S EXHIBIT LIST

To Respondent DAISY DUCK and her attorneys of record,

PLEASE TAKE NOTICE that Petitioner DAFFY DUCKhereby submits the following exhibit list for evidence to be considered at Trial set for 11/29 and 11/30/2022 in Department Z– Honorable Scooby Doo of the Los Angeles Superior Court located at 6230 Sylmar Avenue, Van Nuys, Ca 91401.

Petitioner reserves the right to amend this list. Petitioner reserves the right to use and introduce additional exhibits that are not listed above in order to rebut and/or impeach Respondent's or Witnesses testimony.

Ex #	Description	Offered	Admitted
001	Letter of Motivation 2016 06 06 regarding purchase of the Sherman Oaks home		
002	Title to Sherman Oaks home		
003	Escrow statement for purchase of the Sherman Oaks Home		
004	Bank statement for offer good faith deposit on the Sherman Oaks home		
005	Scrooge McDuck tracing showing Petitioner's down payment on the Sherman Oaks home		
006	Shows transfers relating to Sherman Oaks home purchase		

LINK TO EXHIBITS TO BE USED FOR ELECTRONIC PRESENTATION AND/OR PRINOUTS

LINK <u>TO A DROPBOX ACCOUNT</u>

DATED: 11/1/2022

____

DAFFY DUCK

PROOF OF SERVICE – CODE OF CIVIL PROCEDURE 1013A(3)
STATE OF CALIFORNIA, COUNTY OF LOS ANGELES

I am employed in the County of Absurdity, State of OZ. I am over the age of eighteen (18) and not a party to the within action; my business address is 213 Main Street Neverland, OZ, 420365

On 11/1/2022 I served the foregoing document described as:

PETITIONER'S EXHIBIT LIST

On the interested parties in this action to:

MICKEY MOUSE, ESQ.

Attorney for Respondent Daisy Duck

( ) by facsimile transmission to the above referenced fax telephone number.

(X) by email to MM@DISNEY.COM

( ) I deposited such envelope in the mail at Neverland, OZ. The envelope was mailed with postage thereon fully prepaid.

( ) I am readily familiar with the firm's practice of collection and processing correspondence for mailing. Under that practice it would be deposited with the United States Postal Service on the same day with postage thereon fully prepaid at Neverland OZ in the ordinary course of business. I am aware that on motion of the party served, service is presumed invalid if postal cancellation date or postal meter date is more than one day after date of deposit for mailing in affidavit.

I declare under penalty of perjury under the laws of the State of California that the above is true and correct.

Date: 11/1/2022 ______________________

GOOFY

DAFFY DUCK
In Pro Per
213 Main Street
Neverland, OZ, 420365

SUPERIOR COURT OF OZ
COUNTY OF ABSURDITY

	}	
DAFFY DUCK	}	
Petitioner	}	**Case NO: 19VEPT2016**
	}	
VS.	}	**PETITIONER'S**
	}	**WITNESS LIST**
DAISY DUCK	}	
Respondent	}	
	}	
	}	

I.
PETITIONER'S WITNESS LIST

To Respondent DAISY DUCK and her attorneys of record,

PLEASE TAKE NOTICE that Petitioner DAFFY DUCK hereby submits the following Witness list for Trial set for 11/29 and 11/30/2022 in Department Z– Honorable Scooby Doo of the Los Angeles Superior Court located at 6230 Sylmar Avenue, Van Nuys, Ca 91401.

Petitioner reserves the right to amend this list. Petitioner reserves the right to use and introduce additional Witnesses that are not listed above in order to rebut and/or impeach Respondent's or Witnesses testimony.

Witness#	Name	Time Estimate	
001	DAFFY DUCK	1 DAY	
002	RESPONDENT	1 DAY	
003	PORKY PIG	2 HOURS	
004	GEORGE THE SHEEPDOG	1 DAY	
005	SCROOGE MCDUCK	1 DAY	
006	SYLVESTER	1 HOUR	

DATED: 11/1/2022

DAFFY DUCK

PROOF OF SERVICE – CODE OF CIVIL PROCEDURE 1013A(3)
STATE OF CALIFORNIA, COUNTY OF LOS ANGELES

I am employed in the County of Absurdity, State of OZ. I am over the age of eighteen (18) and not a party to the within action; my business address is 213 Main Street Neverland, OZ, 420365

On 11/1/2022 I served the foregoing document described as:

PETITIONER'S WITNESS LIST

On the interested parties in this action to:

MICKEY MOUSE, ESQ.
Attorney for Respondent Daisy Duck

( ) by facsimile transmission to the above referenced fax telephone number.

(X) by email to MM@DISNEY.COM

( ) I deposited such envelope in the mail at Neverland, OZ. The envelope was mailed with postage thereon fully prepaid.

( ) I am readily familiar with the firm's practice of collection and processing correspondence for mailing. Under that practice it would be deposited with the United States Postal Service on the same day with postage thereon fully prepaid at Neverland OZ in the ordinary course of business. I am aware that on motion of the party served, service is presumed invalid if postal cancellation date or postal meter date is more than one day after date of deposit for mailing in affidavit.

I declare under penalty of perjury under the laws of the State of California that the above is true and correct.

Date: 11/1/2022

____

GOOFY

DAD'S EVIDENCE SCRIPTS

How To Turn an EXHIBIT in EVIDENCE

1. MARK AND IDENTIFY AN EXHIBIT

"I'd like to Mark and Identify Petitioner's / Respondent's 1 as a series of texts between the parties."

2. SHOW THE EXHIBIT TO THE WITNESS

"Do you recognize these texts?"
"Yes."

"Is this a text exchange between you and me?"
"Yes"

"Your honor I offer Exhibit 1 into evidence."

Judge asks Opposing Side
"Any objection?"

USUALLY THERE IS NO OBJECTION.

WHEN THE OTHER SIDE OBJECTS TO AN EXHIBIT

The 2 Most Common objections are:

A. Lack of Foundation
B. Relevance

3. RESPOND TO THE OBJECTION BY:

A. Laying more of a Foundation
(Who, What, When, Why, Where, How)

B. "As an offer of proof your honor
this goes to gatekeeping by the other party."

4. JUDGE ADMITS THE EXHIBIT AND IT'S NOW CALLED EVIDENCE

They'll decide how much to rely on it, how much weight and/or relevance to give it.

How To Lay a Foundation for an EXHIBIT in EVIDENCE

1. TEXT MESSAGES

"I'd like to Mark and Identify Petitioner's / Respondent's 1 as a series of texts between the parties."

SHOW THE EXHIBIT TO THE WITNESS

"Do you recognize these texts?"
"Yes."

"Is this a text exchange between you and me?"
"Yes"

"Your honor I offer Exhibit 1 into evidence."

IF THEY DENY THE TEXTS:

SHOW THE EXHIBIT TO THE WITNESS

"Do you recognize these texts?"
"No."

"Is this a text exchange between you and me?"
"No."

NOW YOU GET THEM TO DENY EVERY ONE OF THE TEXTS
"Didn't you send me a text telling me...
(SOME FACT FROM THE EXCHANGE)

2. PICTURES

"I'd like to Mark and Identify Petitioner's / Respondent's 1 as a true and accurate picture of my child's room in my apartment that I took on March 21, 2024."

A picture is authenticated by SOMEONE who was present when it was taken saying it is a TRUE AND ACCURATE PICTURE on the DATE it was TAKEN.

3. EMAILS

"I'd like to Mark and Identify Petitioner's / Respondent's 1 as an email thread between the parties."

When the witness is on the stand, ask them:
"Is this your email address?" - POINTING to their address
"Do you know that this is MY ADDRESS?" - Point to your address

"Please read the 4th paragraph down, beginning with..."

4. VIDEO

“I’d like to Mark and Identify Petitioner’s / Respondent’s 1 as a video of me being attacked by Pet/Res.”

“Your honor I’d like to play a portion of a video that was recorded on March 24, 2024 from my back door Ring camera. I have provided the other side a copy of the video and a transcript that I have here. I’d liek to start at minute 2:04 and play to 4;30 showing the Respondent breaking into my house.”

5. VOICEMAIL

“I’d like to Mark and Identify Petitioner’s / Respondent’s 1 as a VOICE MAIL RECORDING left by the RESPONDENT on my mobile phone. I have provided the opposing side with a copy of it, and a transcript, which I have given to the court to review.

I have known the RESPONDENT for (however long) and I recognize their voice. They have left me many messages over that time.”

The Kid Inventory

What do you know about your kid? Here are 123 prompts to get you thinking about how well you know your child. You will NOT know all of them, and that's okay, this is just an exercise to get you started.

Briefly, list what you know about your child:

1 Activities that excite them

2 Allergies (food)

3 Allergies (medical)

4 Any nicknames they like

5 Any pets they want or have

6 Any phobias

7 Any secret talents

8 Any special needs or conditions

9 Areas they struggle with academically

10 Bedtime routine

11 Best birthday party theme

12 Best childhood friend

13 Best class project

14 Best compliment they've received

15 Best costume they've worn

16 Academic Strengths

17 Best friend's favorite food

18 Best friend's name

19 Best friend's parents' names

20 Best part of their day

21 Best rainy day activity

22 Best school award

23 Best school subject

24 Best sibling bonding activity

25 Best summer camp memory

26 Best talent

27 Best trick or treat memory

28 Best vacation experience

29 Best way to calm their nerves

30 Best way to celebrate achievements

31 Best way to cheer them up

32 Best way to comfort them

33 Best way to help them study

34 Best way to make them feel loved

35 Best way to make them laugh

36 Best way to spend a Saturday

37 Best way to spend a sunny day

38 Best way to surprise them

39 Best way to wind down before bed

40 Birthday

41 Clothing size

42	Comforting words that work best
43	Favorite art supplies
44	Favorite bedtime prayer
45	Favorite bedtime story
46	Favorite board game
47	Favorite book
48	Favorite breakfast cereal
49	Favorite character from a book
50	Favorite comic book series
51	Favorite educational TV show
52	Favorite fairy tale
53	Favorite family movie night snack
54	Favorite fast food restaurant
55	Favorite food
56	Favorite fruit
57	Favorite game
58	Favorite holiday
59	Favorite kind of pasta dish
60	Favorite local restaurant
61	Favorite movie
62	Favorite outdoor game
63	Favorite park
64	Favorite piece of clothing

65	Favorite school teacher
66	Favorite sea animal
67	Favorite soup
68	Favorite sport
69	Favorite teacher
70	Favorite thing to collect
71	Favorite thing to cook
72	Favorite TV show
73	Favorite type of candy
74	Favorite type of movie
75	Favorite type of pasta
76	Favorite type of pet
77	Favorite YouTube channels
78	What their fears are
79	How they deal with failure
80	How they express anger
81	How they handle being sick
82	How they handle boredom
83	How they handle disappointment
84	How they handle losing
85	How they handle stress
86	How they like to be cheered up
87	Preferred bedtime routine

88	Preferred bedtime story genre
89	Preferred type of cereal
90	Preferred type of cheese
91	Preferred type of cookies
92	Preferred type of dessert
93	Preferred type of exercise
94	Preferred type of fruit juice
95	Preferred type of milkshake
96	Preferred type of music
97	Preferred type of physical activity
98	Preferred type of pie
99	Preferred type of pizza
100	Preferred type of sandwich
101	Preferred type of soup
102	Preferred way to deal with conflict
103	Preferred writing utensil
104	Shoe size
105	Strengths
106	Their bedtime fears or concerns
107	Their definition of fun
108	Their worst habit
109	Things that make them feel special
110	What calms them down

111	What makes them cry
112	What makes them feel brave
113	What makes them feel important
114	What makes them feel loved
115	What makes them feel safe
116	What makes them giggle
117	What makes them laugh
118	What they dislike about school
119	What they dream about
120	What they like about school
121	What they like to read or be read to
122	Worst time of day for them
123	What they like to read

This list is just a beginning place, I have another 300 questions, and I'm sure you can find even more things that I haven't thought about. But this is where you start pulling together what you know about your child so that you can show the judge you've been involved, and if you need to up your game, here's a good place to start!

OTHER BOOKS BY DAVID PISARRA

A Man's Guide To Divorce Strategy
A Man's Guide To Child Custody
A Man's Guide To Domestic Violence
What About Wally? Co-parenting a Pet with An Ex

For speaking engagements, interviews or to contact David Pisarra, email David@DadsLawSchool.com

Made in United States
Cleveland, OH
04 November 2026

47638836R00087